Amazon Fire Phone

All You Need to Know About the First Ever Smartphone from Amazon

Disclaimer

No part of this eBook can be transmitted or reproduced in any form including print, electronic, photocopying, scanning, mechanical, or recording without prior written permission from the author.

All information, ideas, and guidelines presented here are for educational purposes only. While the author has taken utmost efforts to ensure the accuracy of the written content, all readers are advised to follow information mentioned here at their own risk. The author cannot be held responsible for any personal or commercial damage caused by misinterpretation of information. All readers are encouraged to seek professional advice when needed.

All the pictures used in this book are selected from the Amazon website; we do not own any of them.

Contents

The Amazon Fire Phone

In this advanced era, we, the consumers, want a Smartphone that keeps surprising us with new and unique features that helps in enriching and improving our Smartphone experience. Is it any surprise that Amazon wanted a taste of the market, now that it has conquered the digital retail market?

Amazon, is one of the most widely used online shopping websites as well as a name that people trust for most of their online shopping needs. The Amazon website is a world on its own, with millions of products based on every customer need. It is not only that it has millions of products to choose from but it also caters to millions of customers. It has become the first stop for most people's virtual needs. They have managed to acquire this trust and built a digital empire by providing excellent services and products that are delivered on time along with amazing after-sales services.

Indeed when one deals with a million and more customers spread all over the world, one learns all there is to learn about consumer demand and on-time supply. Amazon gathered their information and inspiration from the large market it handle; therefore, 'the result of 'The Amazon Fire Phone' has features that are actually quite unique and have never been seen before in any Smartphone. Amazon is already an expert in providing a range of foolproof services. Now let's take a look at what kind of features it has in store for the Amazon Fire Phone users.

The Three Unique Features

Although Amazon is providing a lot of bonus offers and features for its consumers, there are three distinct features the phone boasts about. Let's take a quick look at the three features, which will be discussed in detail further in the book.

Dynamic Perspective

With the Dynamic Perspective feature, the users of Amazon Fire Phone will be able to experience interactions, which are not possible if they are using any other Smartphone on the market. This feature allows users to tilt, swivel, auto-scroll, and peek in order to access and navigate through the menu and shortcuts with the use of just one hand. This feature allows you to enhance your interaction in games, allowing you to glimpse in hidden corners as well as obstacles using the character's view. It also allows you to use this feature to look through products when using the Amazon shopping app, giving you a better and more detailed view of

Peek to show Yelp
ratings in Maps

products such as clothing, gadgets and what not.

Firefly technology

Using this feature, users can find, with the press of a button, web addresses, email addresses, bar codes, phone numbers, and QR codes. It doesn't only include those but a 100 million other items such as titles of movies, name of TV episodes, the singer, title and album of any song, and any other information you want on any product that is on the screen. By simply pressing the firefly button, you will be able to find a whole lot of information about anything from songs, to movies to products, to people and so on, with only a touch of a button.

Mayday

Mayday is another one of the main features available on the Amazon Fire Phone that allows a user to access free of cost, live video support from an expert, any time of the day and year by simply pressing the right button. You don't have to make any prior appointments, all you need is access to Internet and you will be able to immediately talk to an Amazon expert on any issue you are facing; they are practically waiting to serve you! Now this is what we call amazing. The Amazon after sales service is a unique feature that comes with the brand name. They sure do know what the users want.

Additional features

Amazon Prime

This is one of the more amazing features of the Amazon Fire phone. Fire phone users receive a full year's usage of their Prime service. What is the Prime service you ask? With Prime service, users can stream as well as download unlimited number of times from the thousands of movies and TV episodes available on Prime Instant Video. They can also listen to and download from over thousands of songs from many playlists available using Prime Music.

Kindle Owners' Lending Library

They can also borrow as many books as they want. Totally free of cost! Beside the 500,000

books available on the 'Kindle Owners' Lending Library', they also get Free of cost 'Two Day

Shipping' on any item they purchase. Although you would have to pay data charges when

accessing the Prime networks over your service providers' network, but you do not have to pay

any charges from Amazon by downloading and accessing the content. The best part is, you can

use it all for free if you have a Wi-Fi connection available. So stream thousands of movies, songs

and TV episodes completely free using your Amazon Fire Phone.

Extend Your Existing Membership

If you already have a year's membership for the Prime network, you do not have to regret

missing out on a year's free service. Amazon will extend your current expiry date by another

year on purchasing the phone, free of charge.

Advanced Camera

Captures Images Using Optical Image Stabilization

The Amazon Fire Phone is equipped with a 13MP camera that has 'optical image stabilization' properties. The 13MP camera has a five-element wide aperture f/2.0 lens that allows you to capture crisp and beautiful images. In many situations, we do not have enough lighting to capture a picture without using the flash option in our devices; however, the Amazon Fire phone has optical image stabilization properties. Using this feature, the phone can keep the camera shutter open for more than four times longer compared to other devices on the market. This allows a reduction in noise and blurring on the picture without the use of flash.

Captures 1080p Video

The Amazon Fire Phone allows you to capture the video of any scene using stunning HD graphics in 1080p at 30 fps regardless of which camera you are using. The front facing or the rear facing camera both provide you with equally beautiful and HD videos that capture the essence of the moment.

Capture Immediately

The Camera button allows you to start the camera application without any hassle, so you do not have to wake the phone from sleep mode, unlock it or enter the password, go to the camera app and wait for it to start. By simply clicking the button on the phone, you can initiate the camera even when the screen is off.

Capture Immediately

Free cloud storage

If that wasn't enough good news, here is another one for Amazon Fire phone users. Amazon gives you free cloud storage for every image you to take using your phone in full resolution, so that you do not ever have to delete another picture again. On top of that, the phone is set to automatically back up all your pictures and videos to Amazon Cloud Drive, so that all of your pictures and videos are saved as soon you capture them. You will be able to access your media files anywhere as long as you are using your Amazon Cloud drive!

Wide Scenes

The Amazon Fire Phone allows you to capture any scene you want, no matter how wide it may be using the panorama setting. Simply by holding down the button that controls the shutter, capture a sequence of shots like in a video sequence, that will be combined together to form one picture. You can even combine any number of images to form a single image in the phone's lenticular mode.

High Dynamic Range

The highly intelligent camera feature suggests when to switch on High Dynamic Range (HDR); you can even set it on auto mode. Using the High Dynamic Range, the phone takes multiple shots of one scene and merges them to make one very detailed and vibrant picture.

Applications

No Smartphone is complete without an array of applications to enhance the experience. This is why the Amazon Fire phone also comes with a wide variety of pre-installed applications and tools that will make using the phone even more of an enriching experience. Along with the built in applications, you can also download any of the free and paid applications from the well-stocked Amazon AppStore.

Sample Applications

Some of the applications that can be downloaded include FIFA 14, AndroZip Root File Manager, Any.Do, Bitdefender Antivirus Free, CineXPlayer, Clean Master, ColorNote Notepad Notes, Color Sheep, Drawing Pad, Dropbox, EasilyDo, Easy Installer, Evernote, Hulu Plus, Pulse News, Spotify, Minecraft – Pocket Edition, Quickoffice Pro, PBS Video, Pinterest, Riptide GP2, eBay, TeamViewer for Remote Control, Twitter, Tumblr, ESPN and many more.

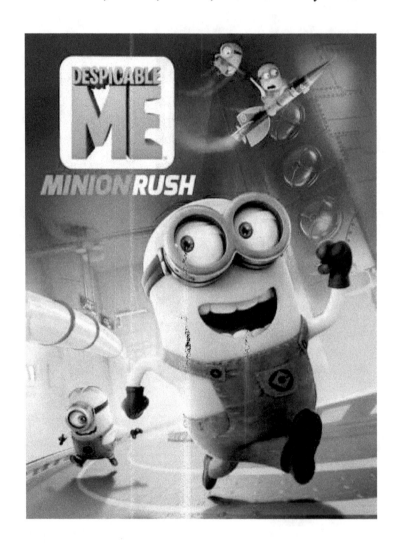

Amazon Coins

Amazon Fire phone also comes equipped with a 1,000 free Amazon Coins, which is valued at $10. Users can spend these coins on applications, games and in-app purchases that will enhance game or app usage experience. Amazon Fire phone users also get a 10% discount when they purchase more Amazon coins.

Home Carousel

When you have the carousel mode activated, you can very efficiently scroll through any application as well as take any action without opening the application. This allows you to control multiple applications directly from the home carousel without leaving the screen. You can check emails, read, delete and arrange them and you can also open your calendar, appointment diary, pictures, websites and so on, directly from the home carousel, saving you a lot of time required in opening and closing each application before moving on to another.

No lag time

The Amazon Fire phone comes equipped with a 2.2 GHz quad-core Snapdragon 800 processor, which is combined with a 2GB RAM. This package makes launching applications faster, allows loading websites in a shorter amount of time and all in all makes this a very fast phone.

Adreno 330 graphics processor

The Adreno 330 graphics processor not only enhances the gaming and media playing experience that gives the phone the fluidity needed for an intense and flexible gaming session. It also allows the Amazon Fire to achieve 3D gaming graphics with a more responsive and complex user interface giving gamers a better experience. Since the Adreno 330 graphics processor performs efficiently by using less power for more workload compared to other graphics processors, this means less charging and more battery life!

Lightning-fast 2.2 GHz
quad-core processor

4G-LTE

The Amazon Fire phone is equipped with nine bands of 4G-LTE along with four bands of GSM as well as five bands of UMTS that allows for better and more impressive voice coverage. It is also gives the phone faster data speeds.

Better view

According to the Amazon website, "The Amazon Fire phone comes equipped with a 4.7 inch HD display. It boasts dynamic contrasts as well as broad viewing angle, circular polarizer, and leading ultra bright display at 590 nits. These altogether makes it amazingly easy to see the screen no matter what the lighting conditions are, whether indoors or outdoors.

Long battery life

One of the most common problems of Smartphone users all over the world is the short battery life. This problem forces them to carry their chargers and portable rechargeable batteries with them wherever they go. However, the Amazon fire phone users wouldn't face this problem at all. The manufacturers claim that the phone comes equipped with superior technology that manages power consumption very efficiently that the battery lasts for many hours. Quoting the website, "the phone delivers around 285 hours of standby time, up to 22 hours of talk time, up to 65 hours of audio playback, and up to 11 hours of video playback."

Sensor system

The Dynamic Perspective technology used in the Amazon Fire phones utilizes four ultra low power superior cameras. They are also the smallest shuttered cameras in the world! It also uses four infrared LEDs for undetectable illumination, real-time computer vision algorithms, and a custom graphics engine rendering at 60 fps.

Swivel for access to important notifications & quick actions

Dolby Digital Plus

The Amazon Fire phone comes equipped with the Dolby Digital Plus technology, which helps in creating an impressive sound experience. The Dolby Digital Plus technology automatically detects the desired volume. Using its built in technology, this feature detects the need to create a virtual surround sound. It helps deliver audio in a quality that is simpler to understand while watching TV shows and movies, eradicating muffling sounds. It automatically chooses the best audio mode according to the activity being carried out on the phone to provide an amazing audio experience.

Tilt to expose right panel: follow along with lyrics for tens of thousands of popular songs

Store Music in cloud

Any of the music tracks or albums that you purchase from Amazon, whether via a laptop, another phone or any other device is easily available on your Fire phone. You can arrange your music by downloading the Amazon Music app on any Smartphone or gadget and then start using it on the Fire phone, when you have it in your hand. You can even download it to play offline by simply tapping the music icon on your home screen.

Tangle-free Headset

The Amazon Fire phone comes with the ultimate headset is designed ergonomically to make it comfortable and easy to wear for the longest of durations. It is also technically tuned to provide as impressive a sound experience as that of the speakers. The headset is created to provide balanced sound with extended bass, which results in very clear voice and audio quality.

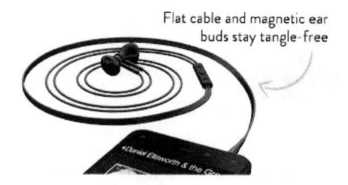

Flat cable and magnetic ear buds stay tangle-free

Amazon Music

You can purchase from over 30 million songs from the Amazon digital music store, from any of your favorite music artist. You can store these files in the free cloud storage provided by the Amazon and stream or download it whenever you want.

Amazon Instant Video

Feel like watching a movie but you do not want to go to the nearest DVD rental place? Or maybe you want to watch a movie on your Smartphone without going through any trouble at all. Guess what! Now you can rent or purchase any TV show or movie from the Amazon Instant Video store. You can either download or stream it to watch whenever you feel like it, no waiting!

Kindle Books

You can find any book you want to read from the millions of available books, magazines and newspapers. Amazon, itself, offers over 500,000 exclusive best-selling titles on the Kindle Books store and app, along with free books that you can read anywhere you want.

Audio books

Sometimes we have no time to read books at all that we would prefer audio versions of our favorite books or the books we want to read. Now you can find thousands of great audio books on the Amazon Fire phone and listen to audio books narrated by popular celebrities and enjoy quality time with actors/actresses you love.

X-Ray

Using the X-Ray technology built into the phone, you can scan any music and find its lyrics on your screen. This will allow users who want sing along with any song they like. Cruise through an extensive library of thousands of songs. You can also get any information on the album, singer and so on, by simply tapping on the screen.

If you want, you can also scan movies and find out in-depth information about the cast, plot synopsis, character information and other such information.

Second Screen

You want to watch a show while you are on the go; you can do so simply by flicking your finger at the screen, which opens up another small screen on the screen that allows you to access the home screen to send messages, make calls or carry out any function you require on the move.

Immersion Reading

To enhance your reading experience, synchronize the eBook you are reading with its audio book, so that you can read and listen to the book at the same time. This can help boost your reading speed considerably. This is best when you are reading in a moving vehicle as it reduces strain on your eyes.

Advanced Streaming and Prediction

Don't we all just hate it when we have to wait for a video to buffer when streaming it? There are probably a few situations as frustrating as waiting for a video to buffer, strictly keeping to the digital experience. With the Amazon Fire phone, you can eradicate buffering from your life forever, and we mean it. The amazing technology within this highly intelligent gadget, allows it to predict what movies or videos you are going to watch that day and it streams them for you, as a result all your videos are already ready to watch. The accuracy of the predictions gets highly precise as you watch more and more, and soon it will adapt to your schedule like your personal helper and prepare what you plan on watching, guessing it accurately every time.

Free backup

Using Amazon Web Services, your phone can be set up to automatically store and back up your settings, applications, notes and other essential information as you change it. You will never have to sit down to backup your settings, as the phone automatically does it for you. This amazing technology allows you to stay worry free, in case your phone is stolen, damaged, or lost.

Wirelessly transfer content from your old device to Fire phone

Whispersync

The amazing Whispersync technology that is equipped in your phone, allows you to easily listen to any audio book while on the move. It also marks where you stopped listening to the audio and saves the settings in the Kindle App. Whenever you play the audio book again, whether in your phone or kindle device, it plays from where you stopped. This technology also remembers where you stopped activity on other applications such as other eBook applications, Video app and so on.

Customized OS

Fire phone is equipped and uses the most up to date version of Fire Operating System. It is an Android system with the added features of cloud service, built-in libraries for media files, a content-forward user interface, apps that boost productivity of the phone and a platform that allows updates to enhance the performance of the phone.

Work as you go

Do you spend a lot of time commuting from work to home, or to other business venues? Your phone allows you to work on the go!

You can edit and review documents, PowerPoint presentations as well as allowing you to stay in touch with what is going on at work, wherever you want. The phone has a built-in Outlook e-mail that allows you to receive emails on the go, keeping you updated about any recent developments at work. You can also manage your appointments directly from your phone and update it to your email or to anyone's email so that they know the changes you have made.

Quick Switch

Do not have time to go through all the apps to find what you are looking for? Simply tap the home button twice to reveal a list or an overlay of the current running apps, allowing you to switch between the applications as easy and quick as 1, 2, and 3.

Collections

Do you like your phone organized?

You can very easily organize all your applications and media files straight from your home

screen into appropriate folders, keeping things so easily organized.

Accessibility features

Users who experience visions problems or old users who have poor sight can find it easier to use the phone with the help of the accessibility tools provided in the Amazon Fire phone. These features allow users to read screen better using the 'Screen Reader' tool, it even allows the user to maneuver the phone better using touch with the help of the tool 'explore by Touch'. They can even magnify the screen, making it easier to read the contents and manage the phone.

1. Power button
2. Headphone jack
3. 2.1MP front-facing camera
4. Dynamic Perspective sensor
5. Home button
6. Micro USB 2.0 port
7. Microphone

8. Dual Stereo Speaker
9. Volume up/down buttons
10. Camera/Firefly button
11. SIM tray
12. 13MP rear-facing camera
13. LED Flash

Made for Fire, case

One of the main focuses of the company was to design phones that are not only full of great technology, tools and features but a phone that is also attractive to look at. For this purpose, Amazon created phone cases for its Fire phone that wouldn't compromise the look of the phone. These form fitting and trendy cases are very sleek, created to fit the phone adding to its look while also providing easy access to all buttons at the same time. These phones are meant to protect the phone against drops and minor accidents.

Bold and Beautiful colors

Although the phone is black in color, the cases are available in bright and stunning colors that allow every user to customize their phones according to their preferences. These cases can be purchased in the following colors:

Premium leather Cases

- Black
- Cayenne

Durable polyurethane

- Black
- Cayenne
- Citron
- Blue
- Royal

Amazon Fire Phone; Is It for You?

We are all excited about the latest gadget from Amazon and the wonderful new features it boasts about. Some of the features such as the 3D view and Firefly are truly remarkable additions to the Smartphone world.

However, what is the not so good bit about this phone?

It's price! The $200 price for the Amazon Fire phone for a two-year contract is pretty steep and ranks on the same level as that of the Samsung Galaxy S5, which is on a level of its own. Most people would expect that Amazon's first release would be charged at a lower price. This would allow a wide array of users to experience the phone and build a liking to it before coming up with a better and more advanced version of the phone that they can price higher.